Recipes by Wm. A. Pizzico,
Gina Marie Corporation

Modern Publishing
A Division of Unisystems, Inc.
New York, New York 10022

Printed in Canada

INTRODUCTION

Convenient Cooking™ is just what the modern cook ordered for quick, easy and delicious food.

Whether you are preparing a simple meal for one, an intimate dinner for two, or a banquet for family or friends, the **Convenient Cooking**™ series will take the work out of planning and preparing your menus, enabling you to enjoy the occasion and the food!

Eight exciting titles provide a convenient recipe center of easy-to-handle, easy-to-read books for every cooking need: meats and ground meats; seafood; chicken and poultry; soups, salads and sauces; omelettes, casseroles and vegetables; microwave meals; desserts; and Cajun food.

Whether you are a beginning cook, or a seasoned food preparer, you will delight in choosing from the range of basic, traditional fare to exotic meals that this series has to offer.

Welcome to the enjoyable and delicious world of **Convenient Cooking.**™

BEEF BURGER PARMESAN

Ingredients:

2 pounds ground beef
1/2 onion, finely
  chopped
2 eggs
3 tablespoons Parmesan
  cheese, grated
1 tablespoon oregano
Salt and pepper to taste
1 cup bread crumbs
1/4 cup cooking oil
1/2 cup mozzarella
  cheese, shredded
2 cups tomato sauce

Directions:

Combine ground beef with onion, 1 egg, grated Parmesan cheese, oregano, salt and pepper. Mix well. Form into hamburger patties. Beat remaining egg in a bowl. Cover hamburger with bread crumbs, dip into egg and coat once again with bread crumbs. Heat cooking oil in large skillet or frying pan. Place burgers into hot oil. Brown 15 minutes on each side. Meanwhile, pour tomato sauce into saucepan. Heat thoroughly. When burgers are done frying, remove from pan and place on paper towels to drain. Arrange onto serving plates. Sprinkle each with mozzarella cheese. Pour hot tomato sauce over top.

Serves: 8 to 10

BEEF ROLLS

Ingredients:

2 pounds ground beef
1 medium onion,
  chopped
Quick-baking biscuit
  dough
Salt and pepper to taste

Directions:

Brown ground beef and onion in skillet. Drain well and let cool slightly. Roll dough into 3 thin rectangles with rolling pin. Spread beef mixture evenly over top of each rectangle. Sprinkle with salt and pepper. Gently gather one side edge of dough and roll lengthwise as you would a jellyroll. Coat beef rolls and baking dish with butter or margarine. Place in a 375°F oven for 30 minutes or until dough is golden brown. Turn occasionally.

Serves: 6

CHEDDAR-BEEF KABOBS

Ingredients:

2 pounds ground beef
1/2 cup barbecue sauce
1 small onion, grated
1/4 cup flour
1 tablespoon mustard
1 teaspoon salt
1/4 teaspoon pepper
1 (10 ounce) stick sharp
  Cheddar cheese
4 large dill pickles, cut
  into 1-inch pieces
Barbecue sauce
Cherry tomatoes

Directions:

Combine ground beef, the 1/2 cup barbecue sauce, onion, flour, mustard, salt and pepper in a medium-sized bowl. Mix lightly. Divide into 24 portions. Cut cheese stick into 24 cubes and wrap meat mixture around cubes. Thread 4 meatballs and 3 dill pickle slices on each of 6 skewers. Refrigerate while heating grill. Grill, 4 inches from heat, 12 to 20 minutes, turning and basting with barbecue sauce. Add 2 cherry tomatoes to each kabob for the last 3 minutes of grilling.

Serves: 6

CHEESY GROUND BEEF AND PASTA

Ingredients:

1/2 pound ground beef
1 (8 ounce) can tomato
  sauce
1 teaspoon oregano
1 clove garlic, minced
Salt and pepper to taste
1/4 pound rotini
  noodles, cooked,
  drained
1/4 cup grated
  Parmesan cheese

Directions:

Brown ground beef in skillet over medium heat, about 5 minutes or until pink is gone. Drain. Add sauce, oregano, garlic, salt and pepper. Cover and simmer over medium-low heat. Stir in rotini. Heat through about 5 minutes and pour onto serving platter. Sprinkle with cheese.

Serves: 4

CHILLI CON CARNE

Ingredients:

2 pounds ground beef
1 medium onion, chopped
1 tablespoon paprika
2 tablespoons chilli powder, mild
1 teaspoon dried basil
1 (15 ounce) can tomatoes, drained
Salt and pepper to taste
1 (15 ounce) can kidney beans

Directions:

Over medium heat, brown ground beef in skillet. Drain. Add onions, paprika, chilli powder, basil, tomatoes, salt and pepper. Cover. Simmer over low heat, 30 minutes, stirring occasionally. Add kidney beans, stir and heat thoroughly. Serve with warm, crusty dinner rolls.

Serves: 2 to 4

CRUNCHY-TOPPED CHEESE BURGERS

Ingredients:

1 pound ground beef
Salt and pepper to taste
1 (8 ounce) jar creamy American cheese
1/2 green pepper, chopped
1 carrot, shredded
1/4 cup mushrooms, sliced

Directions:

Combine ground beef, salt and pepper. Shape into 8 round patties. Place on rack of broiler pan. Broil 7 minutes on each side or until cooked through. Meanwhile melt cheese in double boiler. Stir in green pepper, carrots and mushrooms. Stir until thoroughly heated. Spoon over burgers. *Options:* To cheese add crushed, fried bacon; sliced olives; chopped cucumber or onions. Arrange on hamburger buns. Cook burger in skillet or on barbecue grill. *Helpful Hints:* Serve with potato salad, homefries or french fries. Pierce center of burgers with fork. If juices run clear, burgers are cooked.

Serves: 8

GRILLED PIZZA BURGERS

Ingredients:

2 pounds ground beef
1/2 teaspoon salt
1 (8 ounce) can pizza
  sauce
8 slices mozzarella
  cheese, halved
1/4 cup grated
  Parmesan cheese
1/4 cup finely chopped
  pepperoni
8 hamburger buns,
  toasted
1 teaspoon oregano
1/4 cup sliced
  pepperoni

Directions:

Combine beef, 3/4 cup of the pizza sauce, Parmesan, 1/4 cup chopped pepperoni, oregano and salt. Shape into 16 thin patties. Grill over medium coals 3 to 4 minutes. Turn and brush with some of the remaining pizza sauce. Top each with a half-slice of mozzarella. Grill 3 to 4 minutes longer. Serve 2 cheese-topped patties in each bun. Top with pepperoni slices and remaining pizza sauce.

Serves: 8

GROUND BEEF FIESTA

Ingredients:

1 1/2 pounds ground
  beef
1 medium onion,
  chopped
1 cup tomato sauce
2 cups macaroni shells,
  medium size

Directions:

Place ground beef and onion in large skillet. Brown beef, over medium heat, until pink disappears. Drain excess fat. Add tomato sauce and bring to a gentle boil. Reduce heat, cover and simmer 30 minutes. Stir in cooked macaroni and heat through.

Serves: 4 to 6

GROUND BEEF STROMBOLI

Ingredients:

2 16-ounce portions frozen bread dough, thawed
1 1/2 pounds ground beef
1/4 cup cooking oil
1/4 cup cornmeal
1/2 cup Parmesan cheese
1/2 pound mushrooms, sliced
1 medium green pepper, chopped
1 medium onion, chopped
1/2 pound Provolone cheese
1 (15 ounce) jar of spaghetti sauce
2 tablespoons milk

Directions:

Brown ground beef in cooking oil and drain. Set aside. After dough has stood 10 minutes, roll 1/2 of it out flat and place on a greased pizza pan, sprinkled with cornmeal. Over the dough, sprinkle 1/2 of the Parmesan cheese, ground beef, mushrooms, peppers, onions, Provolone cheese, spaghetti sauce and the remaining Parmesan cheese. Roll out the other 1/2 of the dough the same way as the first 1/2 and place over the entire pie. Pinch edges together like a pie crust, cutting small slits on top. Bake at 400°F for 15 minutes. Brush top of crust with milk and then sprinkle with a little cornmeal. Bake 15 minutes more. Once out of the oven, let stand for 15 minutes before slicing.

Serves: 2 to 4

SURPRISE BURGERS

Ingredients:
2 pounds ground chuck
1/3 cup catsup
2 teaspoons salt
1 tablespoon
  horseradish
4 teaspoons pepper
4 Kaiser rolls
4 cups butter or
  margarine
1 clove garlic, minced
1/2 teaspoon onion salt
Fillings:
4 thin slices onion;
or 4 slices cheese;
or 8 olives, sliced;
or 1/2 cup well-drained
  sauerkraut

Directions:
Mix chuck, salt and pepper. Shape meat into 8 burgers, each about 1/2 inch thick. Top 4 of the burgers with your choice of the fillings. Cover with remaining burgers and pinch edges together. Grill burgers 10 to 12 minutes on each side. Split the Kaiser rolls and place cut side down on grill rack. Grill for 2 minutes. Melt the butter and stir in the garlic and onion salt. Turn the rolls and brush toasted side with garlic butter. Toast 2 minutes and brush other side with butter. Place burgers on bottoms of rolls. Top with mixture of catsup and horseradish.

Serves: 4

MEATBALL KABOBS

Ingredients:
1/2 pound ground beef
1/4 cup bread crumbs,
  seasoned
1 egg, beaten
2 tablespoons water
2 medium tomatoes,
  sliced in 12 wedges
12 cucumber wedges
12 pineapple chunks

Directions:
Combine ground beef, bread crumbs, egg and water. Mix thoroughly. Shape into balls, 1-inch around. Fry meatballs over medium heat, turning, until all sides are browned well. Reduce heat and continue frying a few minutes until cooked through. Remove the meatballs from pan and place on paper towels to drain. Immediately, arrange meatballs on 6-inch skewers, alternating with tomato wedges, cucumber wedges and pineapple chunks.

Serves: 6

MEATBALL STEW

Ingredients:

1 1/2 pounds ground beef

1 (10 1/2 ounce) can tomato soup, condensed

1 cup bread crumbs

1 (10 1/2 ounce) can beef broth, condensed

1/4 cup onions, finely chopped

4 medium potatoes, pared and quartered

1 egg beaten

4 carrots, cut into 1-inch slices

1 teaspoon salt

3 small white onions, peeled

1/2 teaspoon marjoram

1/2 teaspoon thyme

2 tablespoons cooking oil

Directions:

Combine ground beef, bread crumbs, onions, egg, salt, marjoram and thyme. Mix and shape into meatballs. Place in Dutch oven with cooking oil and brown on all sides. Drain away oil. Combine soup and broth and add to meatballs. Also add potatoes, carrots and onions. Bring to a boil. Cover and reduce heat. Simmer 30 minutes or until vegetables are tender.

Serves: 6 to 8

MEATLOAF A LA BILL

Ingredients:

2 pounds ground beef
1 medium onion, chopped
1 egg, beaten
1/4 cup Parmesan cheese, grated
1/2 cup bread crumbs
1 cup water
4 tablespoons flour

Directions:

Combine ground beef, onion, egg, cheese, bread crumbs and four tablespoons of the water. Mix well, place in a baking pan and shape into a loaf. Cover and bake in a 350° F oven for 1 hour. Remove the meatloaf to a platter and drain excess fat from the pan. Mix remaining water with flour. When mixture is smooth, add to the drippings in the pan. Stir until thick and bubbly. Pour over sliced meatloaf.

Serves: 4

TEMPTING TACOS

Ingredients:
1 pound ground beef
2 tablespoons paprika
1 tablespoon chilli
 powder
1 teaspoon garlic
 powder
Salt and pepper to taste
3/4 cup water
10 taco shells
3/4 cup mozzarella
 cheese, shredded
1 cup lettuce, chopped
2 medium tomatoes,
 chopped

Directions:
Brown ground beef in skillet. Drain well. Add paprika, garlic powder, chilli powder, salt and pepper and water. Stir, cover and simmer 10 minutes. Fill taco shells half way. Layer cheese, lettuce and tomato over top.

Serves: 10

TEXAS CHILLI WITH BEANS

Ingredients:
1 tablespoon cooking
 oil
1 pound ground beef
1 (16 ounce) can
 tomatoes
1 (10 ounce) can kidney
 beans
1 (4 ounce) can mild
 chilli peppers,
 chopped
1 tablespoon paprika
Salt and pepper to taste

Directions:
Pour cooking oil in skillet. Add ground beef and simmer over medium heat until browned. Drain. Stir in tomatoes, beans, peppers, paprika, salt and pepper. Cover and simmer 20 minutes. *Options:* Add Tabasco sauce for hot chilli. Sauce can be used in place of tomatoes for a saucier chilli. *Helpful Hints:* Serve in taco shells, with nacho chips, tortillas or alone.

Serves: 4 to 6

SALISBURY STEAKS WITH MUSHROOM GRAVY

Ingredients:
2 pounds ground beef
3 tablespoons butter or margarine
2 eggs, slightly beaten
1 tablespoon cooking oil
1 teaspoon salt
1 tablespoon water
1/4 teaspoon pepper
3 tablespoons flour
1/3 cup bread crumbs
1 1/3 cups beef broth
1/4 pound fresh mushrooms, sliced

Directions:
Combine beef, eggs, salt and pepper in mixing bowl. Stir gently with fork. Shape mixture into 6 oval size steaks, about 1/2 inch thick and 5 inches long. Sprinkle both sides with bread crumbs and press them firmly into steaks. Refrigerate until well chilled, about 45 minutes. In a skillet, sauté mushrooms in melted butter until lightly brown and remove. Place remaining butter or margarine and oil into same skillet and heat. Add steaks and fry about 2 minutes on each side until bread crumb coating is golden brown and crispy. Prepare gravy by adding cold water to flour and stirring until smooth. Add flour mixture to pan juices along with broth and mushrooms. Bring to boil. Reduce heat and stir until gravy thickens.

Serves: 6

QUICK MINI-PIZZAS

Ingredients:
1 pound ground beef
1 small onion, chopped
6 English muffins
1 1/4 cup tomato sauce
3/4 cups mozzarella cheese, shredded

Directions:
Brown ground beef and onion in frying pan. Drain well. Split English muffins in half and place on cookie sheet. Layer each half with 1 tablespoon of sauce, ground beef, then top with cheese. Add remaining sauce evenly over top of cheese. Place in a 350°F oven for 10 minutes or until cheese is melted and bubbly.

Serves: 12

STUFFED BURGERS

Ingredients:
1 cup packaged herb-seasoned stuffing mix
1/4 cup chopped celery
1/4 chopped onion
1 tablespoon parsley
1/4 cup milk
1 teaspoon lemon juice
2 teaspoons Worcestershire sauce
1 1/2 pounds ground beef
1/2 teaspoon salt

Directions:
Prepare stuffing mix according to package directions. Stir in parsley and lemon juice; set aside. Combine beef with celery, onion, milk, Worcestershire and salt. Shape meat mixture into 12 thin patties. Spoon 2 tablespoons stuffing mixture onto 6 of the patties. Top with remaining patties and seal edges. Grill over medium hot coals 8 to 10 minutes. Turn and grill 6 to 8 minutes longer or until done.

Serves: 6

SUPER SLOPPY JOES

Ingredients:
1 pound ground beef
1 (16 ounce) can tomatoes whole, drained
1 medium onion, chopped
1 small green pepper, chopped
1 tablespoon paprika
1 tablespoon chilli powder
Salt and pepper to taste
4 to 6 hamburger rolls

Directions:
Brown ground beef in a skillet. Add onions and peppers and let simmer for 10 minutes. Add tomatoes, paprika, chilli powder and salt and pepper to taste. Let simmer for an additional 5 minutes. Serve over rolls *Options:* Shredded beef may also be used with this recipe.

Serves: 4 to 6

SUPER SWISS STEAK

Ingredients:
2 pounds ground steak
1/4 cup flour
3 tablespoons cooking oil
1 (16 ounce) can tomatoes, undrained
1 large onion, sliced
1/2 cup celery, chopped
Salt and pepper to taste

Directions:
Shape ground steak into oval patties. Sprinkle with flour, place in hot oil and brown quickly on both sides. Drain. Combine tomatoes, onion, celery, salt and pepper in bowl. Pour over steak. Cover and simmer over low heat, 25 minutes. Remove steaks to platter and pour tomato mixture over top.

Serves: 6

HERBED BEEF BURGERS

Ingredients:
1 pound ground beef
1/4 cup beef broth
1 clove garlic, minced
1/2 teaspoon allspice
1/2 teaspoon thyme
1/2 teaspoon oregano
Salt and pepper to taste

Directions:
Combine ground beef, broth, garlic, allspice, thyme, oregano, salt and pepper. Mix well. Shape into 4 patties. Arrange on rack of broiler pan. Broil 7 minutes on each side or until cooked through. *Options:* Add chopped onion, celery or green pepper. Pour brown gravy over broiled burgers. This ground beef can be made into herbed meatballs, then fried. *Helpful Hints:* Broiling time depends on thickness of burger; flat, wide patties will cook in less time than thick, round burgers. Pierce center of burger with fork to see if juices run clear. This insures doneness. Serve with boiled potatoes and mixed vegetables.

Serves: 4

BACON WRAPPED VEAL

Ingredients:
4 strips bacon
4 veal cutlets
1 onion, chopped
1 cup brown beef gravy

Directions:
Fry bacon in skillet until thoroughly cooked, but not crisp. Remove from pan and drain on paper towels. Add veal and onions to same skillet. Brown lightly on both sides, about 10 minutes on each side. Remove from skillet. Carefully wrap bacon around each cutlet. Place back in pan. Pour gravy over top. Cover and simmer 10 minutes over medium-low heat or until gravy is hot and bubbly.

Serves: 4

VEAL CORDON BLEU

Ingredients:
4 veal cutlets (3 ounces each)
4 thin slices smoked, sliced ham
4 thin slices Swiss cheese
2 tablespoons flour
1/2 teaspoon salt
1/4 teaspoon pepper
1/4 teaspoon ground allspice
1 egg, slightly beaten
1/2 cup bread crumbs
3 tablespoons shortening
2 tablespoons water

Directions:
Pound veal to 1/4-inch thick. Place 1 slice each of ham and cheese on each piece of veal. Roll up carefully, beginning at the narrow end. Secure with wooden toothpicks. Mix flour, salt, pepper and allspice. Coat rolls with flour mixture. Dip rolls into egg. Then roll in bread crumbs. Heat shortening in a 10-inch skillet until melted. Cook rolls in shortening until brown, about 8 minutes. Add water. Heat to boiling; reduce heat, cover and simmer until veal is tender, about 45 minutes. Remove cover during last 2-3 minutes to crisp veal slightly.

Serves: 4

LEMON-TARRAGON VEAL CHOPS

Ingredients:

2 veal chops, cut 1/2 inch thick

1 (2 ounce) can sliced mushrooms

2 teaspoons butter or margarine

1/3 cup skim milk

1 1/2 teaspoons cornstarch

2 teaspoons lemon juice

1/4 teaspoon salt

Dash tarragon

Dash pepper

Directions:

Place chops on broiler pan rack. Broil 3 to 4 inches from heat for 5 minutes. Turn chops, sprinkle with salt and pepper. Broil about 5 minutes more or until done. Meanwhile, in saucepan combine undrained mushrooms and butter. Cook over low heat until butter is melted. In screw-top jar combine milk and cornstarch; shake well. Add to mushrooms. Cook and stir over medium heat until thickened and bubbly. Remove from heat. Stir in lemon juice, salt, tarragon and pepper. Spoon sauce over chops.

Serves: 2

SAUCY VEAL CHOPS

Ingredients:
6 veal chops, 1/2 inch
 thick
1/2 cup flour
2 tablespoons cooking
 oil
1/2 cup tomato sauce
1 tablespoon oregano

Directions:
Coat veal with flour. Heat cooking oil in skillet and place veal into hot oil. Lightly brown each side. Add tomato sauce and oregano. Cover and simmer over low heat for 45 minutes or until veal is tender.

Serves: 6

SAUTÉED TENDERLOIN OF VEAL

Ingredients:
3 tablespoons olive oil
2 pounds veal
 tenderloin, cut into
 bite-size cubes
1 (10 ounce) can
 mushroom caps;
 reserve liquid
1/4 cup dry white wine
2 beef bouillon cubes
1 clove garlic, minced
1/2 teaspoon thyme
Salt and pepper to taste

Directions:
Heat olive oil in skillet. Add veal and sauté over medium-high heat, stirring. Evenly brown on all sides. Reduce heat and continue sautéing until cooked through. Add mushrooms, reserved liquid, wine, bouillon cubes, garlic, thyme, salt and pepper. Simmer until liquid boils down to 1/2 the original amount, about 20 minutes.

Serves: 4 to 6

TENDER VEAL AND SAUSAGE WRAPS

Ingredients:
6 sausage patties, small
2 pounds veal cutlets, cut thin
1/2 cup flour
3 cups canned tomatoes; reserve liquid
1 small onion, chopped
1 tablespoon Worcestershire sauce
2 teaspoons garlic powder
Salt and pepper to taste

Directions:
In large skillet, brown sausages on both sides. Meanwhile, place veal between two pieces of wax paper and flatten with rolling pin. Wrap sausage with veal and secure with toothpicks. Coat veal with flour and place into pan with fat from sausage. Brown lightly on all sides. Drain. In pan add tomatoes, reserved liquid, onion, Worcestershire sauce, garlic powder, salt and pepper. Stir mixture, gently scraping bottom of pan to loosen drippings, if any. Cover and simmer 45 minutes or until veal is tender.

Serves: 4 to 6

SUPER SCALLOPINI

Ingredients:
1 pound veal cutlets
1/2 cup Parmesan cheese
3 tablespoons butter
1 tablespoon cooking oil
1 clove garlic
1/4 cup beef stock
1/4 cup red wine

Directions:
Pound veal thin with small meat cleaver. Cut into cubes. Coat veal with Parmesan cheese. Heat butter and oil in skillet. Add garlic and veal. Cook 15 minutes, browning all sides. Remove garlic and veal from skillet. Arrange veal on platter, keeping warm. Turn heat to medium-high. Add stock and stir, scraping bottom of pan. Cook 1 minute. Add wine and cook 1 minute more. Pour over veal.

Serves: 3

STUFFED VEAL ROLLS

Ingredients:
6 veal cutlets
1/4 cup butter or
    margarine
2 tablespoons Parmesan
    cheese, grated
Salt and pepper to taste
1 1/4 cups bread
    stuffing

Directions:
Place veal between 2 pieces of wax paper. Roll with rolling pin until well flattened. Brush with 1/2 of butter or margarine and sprinkle with cheese, salt and pepper. Place 2 tablespoons stuffing on edge of each cutlet. Roll up as you would a jellyroll, securing with toothpicks. Add veal rolls and remaining butter or margarine to frying pan and heat. Brown lightly on all sides. Remove veal to baking dish and place in a 350°F oven for 20 minutes or until done.

Serves: 6

VEAL AND SPINACH SURPRISE

Ingredients:
1 pound veal cutlets,
    cut in serving pieces
2 tablespoons butter
2 tablespoons flour
3/4 cup milk
1/8 teaspoon nutmeg
Salt and pepper to taste
1 bunch spinach,
    cooked, drained well
1/4 cup Parmesan
    cheese, grated
1/2 teaspoon paprika

Directions:
Flatten veal with rolling pin and set aside. Combine butter and flour in skillet and mix well until smooth. Gradually add milk and cook slowly over low heat, stirring constantly. When mixture has thickened, stir in nutmeg, salt and pepper. Arrange veal in baking dish. Place an even amount of spinach on each veal cutlet. Pour sauce over top. Sprinkle cheese and paprika over top. Place in a 350°F oven for 30 minutes.

Serves: 4

VEAL BATTER-FRIED

Ingredients:
8 veal steaks, 1/2 inch
  thick
1 teaspoon garlic
  powder
Salt and pepper to taste
1/4 cup cooking oil
1 cup flour
3/4 cup Parmesan
  cheese, grated
2/3 cup flat beer
1 teaspoon olive oil
3 eggs, beaten

Directions:
Roll veal with rolling pin until thin. Season with garlic, salt and pepper. Heat cooking oil in skillet. Meanwhile, combine flour, cheese, beer, olive oil and eggs. Mix well. Dip each veal steak into batter and place into hot cooking oil. Fry 10 minutes on each side until golden brown and cooked through. Drain on paper towels.

Serves: 6

VEAL CROQUETTES

Ingredients:
2 cups cooked veal,
  chopped
Salt and pepper to taste
1/8 teaspoon cayenne
Few drops of onion
  juice or 1/3
  teaspoon onion salt
3 eggs
1 cup thick white
  cream sauce
1 cup bread crumbs
1/4 cup cooking oil

Directions:
Combine cooked veal, salt, pepper, cayenne, onion juice and 1 egg. Once completely mixed, add the cream sauce a little at a time until mixture becomes moist. Have mixture soft enough so the croquettes can be easily handled when shaped. This will make them soft and creamy inside. Shape by rolling a tablespoonful of mixture between your hands into a ball. Flatten the bottoms and arrange in desired shape. Roll each first into bread crumbs, then into remaining eggs, and then into the bread crumbs once again. Fry in hot cooking oil on top of the stove in a heavy frying pan or at 300°F in a deep fryer until deep golden brown (if using a deep fryer more oil will be needed). Drain on paper towels and arrange on a serving dish, but do not cover.

Serves: 4

VEAL CURRY

Ingredients:
1 pound veal chops,
  1/2 inch thick
2 onions, sliced
2 tablespoons butter or
  margarine
1 1/2 teaspoons curry
  powder
3/4 cup water
2 tablespoons flour
3 cups cooked rice

Directions:
In medium-high skillet, sear veal 2 minutes on each side. Cut veal into 1 1/2-inch pieces. Remove veal from skillet. Add onion and butter. Sauté 2 minutes stirring or until onions brown. Place veal back in skillet. Sprinkle with curry powder and pour water over top. Stir in flour. Cover and simmer until gravy thickens, 5 minutes. Stir often. Serve over rice.

Serves: 4

VEAL CUTLETS

Ingredients:
2 tablespoons cooking
  oil
1/2 cup butter
1 pound veal cutlets
1/2 cup grated
  Parmesan cheese
1 egg, beaten
1 cup bread crumbs

Directions:
Heat oil in frying pan. Meanwhile, melt butter and pour in bowl. Dip veal in butter, coat with egg and roll in mixture of grated cheese and bread crumbs. Place in oil. Over medium heat fry 8 minutes on each side, or until golden brown and cooked through.

Serves: 4

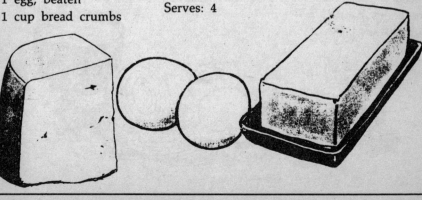

VEAL A LA ORANGE

Ingredients:
4 veal chops, 1/2 inch thick
1 garlic clove, chopped
Salt and pepper to taste
1 teaspoon basil
4 oranges, peeled and cut into bite size pieces

Directions:
Rub veal with garlic, salt and pepper. Place on rack of broiler pan. Broil 8 minutes on each side. Meanwhile, heat oranges and basil in a saucepan. Place veal on a platter and pour oranges over top.

Serves: 2 to 4

VEAL A LA SOUR CREAM

Ingredients:
2 pounds veal, cut into 1-inch pieces
1/2 cup flour
4 tablespoons cooking oil
1 small onion, sliced thin
1/4 cup mushrooms, sliced
2 teaspoons paprika
1 cup instant beef bouillon
3/4 cup sour cream
1/4 cup pimentos

Directions:
Coat veal with flour. Heat cooking oil in skillet and brown veal on both sides. Add onion and mushrooms. Simmer until just tender. Stir in paprika and bouillon. Cover and simmer 20 minutes or until veal is tender. Add sour cream and pimentos. Mix thoroughly and heat through. Do not boil.

Serves: 4

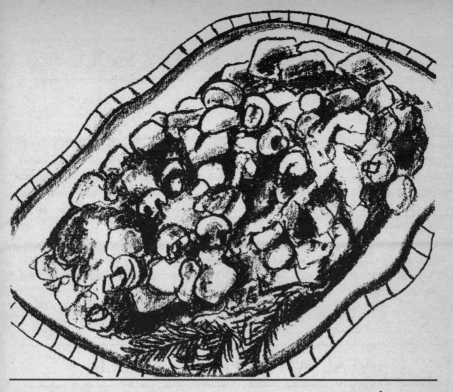

VEAL PAPRIKA A LA CONSOMMÉ

Ingredients:
1/2 cup flour
2 teaspoons paprika
Salt and pepper to taste
1 1/2 pounds veal, cut into serving pieces
3 tablespoons cooking oil
1 large onion, sliced
1 cup consommé
1 teaspoon garlic powder
1/2 cup sliced mushrooms

Directions:
Combine flour, paprika, salt and pepper. Coat veal with flour mixture. Heat 2 tablespoons cooking oil in large skillet. Add veal and lightly brown on each side. Remove veal from skillet and set aside. Add remaining oil, onions and mushrooms to same skillet and sauté until onions are transparent. Return veal to skillet. Stir in consommé and garlic powder. Cover and simmer 30 minutes or until tender.

Serves: 4 to 6

VEAL STEAKS IN SHERRY SAUCE

Ingredients:

1 1/2 pounds veal steaks, cut into serving pieces
Salt and pepper to taste
1/2 cup bread crumbs
2 tablespoons butter or margarine
1/4 cup beef bouillon
3 tablespoons dry cooking sherry

Directions:

Flatten each veal steak by rolling gently with rolling pin. Season both sides with salt and pepper. Coat with bread crumbs. Melt butter or margarine in large skillet. Add veal and brown 15 minutes on both sides or until cooked through. Remove from skillet and set aside. Add sherry and beef bouillon and heat. Stir, scraping bottom of skillet to loosen drippings. When sauce is hot, pour over veal steaks.

Serves: 4

VEAL WITH SPINACH SAUCE

Ingredients:

4 veal cutlets
1/2 cup flour
Salt and pepper to taste
Olive oil, enough to cover bottom of pan
2 cups noodles, cooked
4 tablespoons butter or margarine
1/4 cup spinach, finely chopped, cooked
2 tablespoons Parmesan cheese, grated

Directions:

Roll veal cutlet with rolling pin to flatten. Coat lightly with flour and sprinkle with salt and pepper. Heat oil in skillet until it begins to bubble. Add veal and quickly brown on both sides. Remove and arrange over noodles. Melt butter or margarine in saucepan. Add spinach and grated cheese. Simmer until heated. Sauce should be slightly thick. Pour over veal and noodles.

Serves: 4

BEEFY BEEF STROGANOFF

Ingredients:

1 pound beef sirloin, cut into strips
1 tablespoon flour
1/2 teaspoon salt
2 tablespoons butter
1 cup mushrooms, sliced
1/2 cup onion, chopped
1 clove garlic, minced
2 tablespoons butter
3 tablespoons flour
1 tablespoon tomato paste
1 1/4 cups beef stock
1 cup dairy sour cream
2 tablespoons cooking sherry

Directions:

Combine 1 tablespoon flour and salt; coat meat strips in mixture. Heat skillet and add 2 tablespoons butter. When melted, add strips and brown quickly on all sides. Add mushrooms, onion and garlic. Cook until onion is just tender. Remove meat and mushrooms from skillet. Add 2 tablespoons butter to drippings and melt. Then blend in 3 tablespoons flour and then tomato paste. Slowly pour in meat stock; cook, stirring constantly and let mixture thicken. Return meat and mushrooms to skillet. Stir in sour cream and sherry; heat briefly. Serve with rice or buttered noodles.

Serves: 4 to 5

BEEF ELEGANTE OVER RICE

Ingredients:

1 1/2 pounds round steak, thinly sliced
1 3/4 cups beef broth
1/2 cup seasoned flour
1 (4 ounce) can sliced mushrooms with liquid
3 tablespoons corn oil
1 cup chopped onions
3 cups hot, cooked rice
1/4 cup dry red wine
Tomato wedges

Directions:

Cut steak into 1-inch strips. Coat strips with seasoned flour; brown in oil. Add onions and cook 2 to 3 more minutes. Stir in wine, broth and mushrooms with liquid; bring to a boil. Cover, reduce heat, and simmer 20 to 30 minutes or until tender. Serve over rice. Garnish with tomato wedges.

Serves: 6

SIRLOIN STEAK FOR TWO

Ingredients:

1 teaspoon garlic
  powder
Salt and pepper to taste
10 ounce sirloin steak

Directions:

Rub garlic, salt and pepper onto both sides of steak. Place on rack of broiler pan. Place in preheated broiler, 4 inches from heat. Cook 7 minutes on each side for medium-done.

Serves: 2

BEEF WITH WINE

Ingredients:

1/4 pound bacon
1 onion, sliced
2 cups Burgundy wine
1 cup water
Salt and pepper to taste
1/2 cup flour
2 pounds lean beef
cubes

Directions:

Fry bacon to desired crispness and drain. In same pan, combine bacon, onion, 1 cup wine, water, salt and pepper and cook over low heat until onions are soft. Remove bacon and onions and set aside. Place flour in a small plastic bag, add meat cubes and shake, coating meat thoroughly. Add to juices in pan along with remaining cup of wine. Simmer 25 minutes on low heat. Add bacon and onions. Heat through.

Serves: 4 to 6

BREADED STEAK CUTLETS

Ingredients:

1 pound cubed steaks,
cut into serving
pieces
2 tablespoons cooking
oil
1 egg, beaten
1 cup bread crumbs,
seasoned
Salt and pepper to taste

Directions:

Heat cooking oil in skillet. Meanwhile, dip steaks in egg and then into bread crumbs. Place in heated oil, sprinkle with salt and pepper and fry over medium heat for 15 minutes on each side (or until golden brown).

Serves: 4

STEAK WITH MUSHROOM WINE SAUCE

Ingredients:

2 tablespoons margarine or butter

1/4 pound mushrooms, thinly sliced

2 tablespoons chopped onion

1 clove garlic, crushed

2 teaspoons flour

2 pounds boneless sirloin steak

1/4 teaspoon salt

Dash pepper

2 tablespoons tomato paste

1/2 cup dry red wine

1/4 cup water

Directions:

Melt margarine or butter in small saucepan over medium heat. Add mushrooms, onion and garlic. Sauté until onion is transparent, stirring frequently. Remove from heat. Stir in flour, salt, pepper and tomato paste. Blend in wine and water. Bring to boil, stirring frequently. Cover, reduce heat, and simmer 20 minutes. Meanwhile broil steak to desired doneness. Serve steak with sauce.

Serves: 6

CHINESE STIR FRY

Ingredients:

1 1/2 to 2 pounds flank steak, cut into strips

2 tablespoons cooking oil

3 medium green peppers, cut into strips

1 clove garlic, minced

3 small tomatoes, cut into wedges

1/4 cup soy sauce

1/4 teaspoon ginger

1/2 teaspoon sugar

1 tablespoon cornstarch

1/4 cup water

Directions:

Combine cornstarch, sugar, ginger and stir into the soy sauce. Pour mixture over meat and stir once again. Quickly brown beef strips and mixture in hot oil and remove from pan. Reduce heat and add green pepper, garlic and water to the pan and cook until peppers are tender, about 5 minutes. Stir in meat and tomatoes and heat through.

Serves: 4

ELEGANT BEEF TENDERLOIN

Ingredients:
4 fillets, 1/2 inch thick
1 tablespoon butter
1/2 cup brandy
1/2 cup sour cream
1 tablespoon catsup
Dash of Worcestershire
  sauce
Salt to taste
Tabasco sauce to taste
Horseradish to taste

Directions:
Place butter in skillet and brown fillets, about 6 to 8 minutes. Remove and place on a warm platter. Pour 1/2 of the brandy over fillets. Mix in the skillet: sour cream, catsup, Worcestershire sauce, salt, Tabasco sauce, horseradish and the other half of the brandy. Heat thoroughly, stirring constantly. Spoon the sauce over the warm steaks and serve.

Serves: 4

FIREHOUSE POT ROAST

Ingredients:
1 3 pound boneless rump roast
2 cans condensed cream of mushroom soup
1 package dried onion soup mix

Directions:
Preheat oven to 325°F. Place roast on double thickness of foil. Pour soup over meat and sprinkle on soup mix. Wrap meat entirely in foil, place in a shallow pan, and cook for 2 1/2 hours until tender. The juices from the meat will blend with the soups and produce a thick, smooth gravy which you can serve on the side.

Serves: 6

FLANK STEAK 'N' BEER

Ingredients:
1/2 cup corn oil
1 teaspoon salt
1/2 cup beer
1 bay leaf
2 tablespoons lemon juice
1/2 teaspoon thyme
2 cloves garlic, crushed
1/8 teaspoon pepper
1 1/2 to 2 pounds flank steak

Directions:
Mix together corn oil, beer, lemon juice, garlic, salt, bay leaf, thyme and pepper. Trim excess fat from flank steak; place in shallow baking dish. Pour marinade over meat; cover and marinate in refrigerator at least 2 hours or overnight, turning several times. Place steak on rack in broiler pan and baste with marinade. Broil 3 to 4 inches from heat 16 to 20 minutes, turning once.

Serves: 6

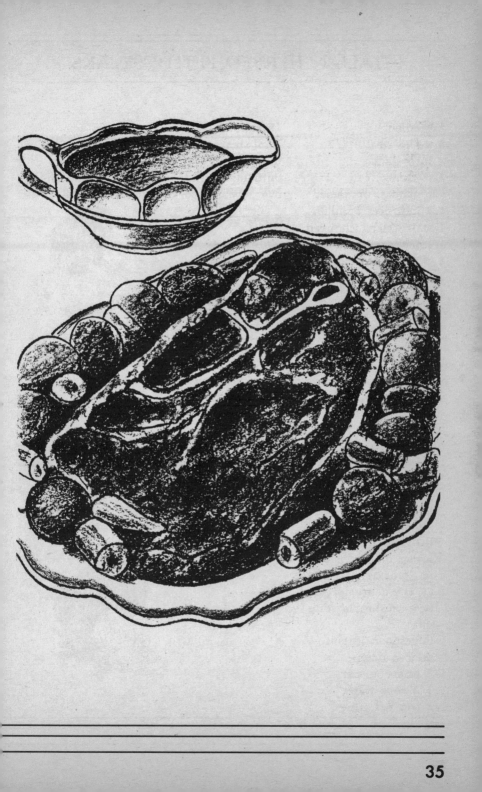

ITALIAN HERBED PETITE STEAKS

Ingredients:

2 petite steaks, 1/2
  inch thick
1 (8 ounce) can
  tomatoes, undrained
1/2 cup beef bouillon
1 stalk celery, chopped
1 small onion, chopped
1 clove garlic, minced
1 teaspoon oregano
1 teaspoon basil
Salt and pepper to taste

Directions:

Broil steaks 4 minutes on each side. Remove to skillet. Add remaining ingredients. Stir until mixed thoroughly. Cover and simmer over low heat for 30 minutes or until tender.

Serves: 2

IT'S A CINCH BEEF BOURGUIGNONNE

Ingredients:

1 1/2 pounds sirloin,
  cut into 1-inch cubes
1/4 teaspoon pepper
1/2 green pepper, cut
  into 1-inch squares
1 tablespoon butter or
  margarine
1/2 cup drained, sliced
  mushrooms
1 (1 1/4 ounce) package
  beef-mushroom soup
  mix
1 tablespoon instant
  minced onion
1/2 teaspoon salt
1 1/2 cups water
1/2 cup red wine

Directions:

In large frying pan, brown meat in butter. Add mushrooms and onion and continue browning until tender. Add remaining ingredients except wine. Simmer, stirring frequently, until sauce thickens. Add wine; continue simmering for 15 to 20 minutes until meat is tender.

Serves: 4 to 6

MINUTE STEAK BORDELAISE

Ingredients:
2 tablespoons butter
2/3 cup dry red wine
1 medium onion, sliced
2 tablespoons sherry
1 clove garlic
Salt to taste
1 cup beef broth or
   bouillon
Pepper to taste
1 tablespoon cornstarch,
   dissolved in 2
   tablespoons water
1 pound minute steaks

Directions:
Melt butter in skillet; cook onion and garlic until tender. Stir in beef broth and dissolved cornstarch. Heat to boiling, stirring until sauce thickens. Stir in red wine and sherry; season with salt and pepper. Pour sauce into saucepan and keep warm. Add minute steaks to original skillet; raise heat and cook, turning occasionally until evenly browned. Remove steaks to serving platter and pour sauce over them.

Serves: 4

BEEF TERIYAKI

Ingredients:
6 slices beef sirloin, 1/4
   to 1/2 inch thick
Teriyaki sauce (see
   recipe)

Directions:
Marinate beef slices in Teriyaki sauce overnight in refrigerator. Turn occasionally. Place on greased grill 6 to 8 inches from hot coals. Turn only once; baste with marinade. Grill 25 minutes for well-done.

Teriyaki Sauce: Mix 1/2 cup soy sauce, 1/4 cup honey, 1/2 teaspoon ginger and 1 clove garlic, minced.

Serves: 6

PARSLEYED OVEN POT ROAST

Ingredients:
1 1/2 teaspoons salt
1/4 teaspoon pepper
1 5-pound bottom
    round roast
1 (1 pound, 12 ounce)
    can tomatoes, broken
    up
3/4 cups dry red wine
1/4 cup instant minced
    onion
2 tablespoons parsley
1 bay leaf
1/2 teaspoon instant
    minced garlic
1 teaspoon salt
6 medium carrots,
    peeled and sliced
1 1/2 pounds zucchini,
    sliced
3 cups cherry tomatoes

Directions:
Rub 1 1/2 teaspoons salt and the pepper into surface of meat. Place meat, fat side down in heavy casserole or Dutch oven. Brown well on all sides in 450°F oven 50 to 60 minutes; drain off fat. Combine tomatoes, wine, minced onion, parsley, bay leaf, minced garlic, and remaining 1 teaspoon salt. Pour over meat. Cover and reduce heat to 350°F. Bake 2 1/2 to 3 hours or until meat and vegetables are tender, adding carrots 40 minutes before cooking time is up, zucchini 20 minutes, and cherry tomatoes 10 minutes before time is up. Slice meat and serve with vegetables.

Serves: 6 to 8

SEASONED LONDON BROIL

Ingredients:
2 tablespoons cooking
    oil
1 pound London Broil-
    style steak
1/4 cup Worcestershire
    sauce
2 teaspoons oregano
Salt and pepper

Directions:
Preheat broiler or barbecue. In bowl mix sauce, oregano, and salt and pepper. Place steak on rack of broiler pan. Brush top side generously with mixture. Broil 7 minutes. Turn steak over, brush sauce on top and continue to broil for an additional 8 minutes.

Serves: 4

SOUTH PHILLY CHEESE STEAKS

Ingredients:
2 tablespoons cooking oil

1 medium onion, sliced thick

1/2 pound prepared steak fillets

Salt and pepper to taste

2 long sandwich rolls

1/2 cup tomato sauce

1/2 cup mozzarella cheese, grated

Directions:
Heat cooking oil in skillet. Add onions and sauté over medium-low heat for 3 minutes or until just tender. Add steak, salt and pepper. Fry until pink disappears. Slice sandwich rolls lengthwise, three-quarters of the way through. Open rolls flat and arrange steak and onions evenly on bottom half of rolls. Spoon tomato sauce over top. Sprinkle with cheese and place in broiler 1 minute or until cheese melts. *Options:* Add green pepper or mushrooms for extra flavor. American cheese also works well in this recipe. Leave steaks whole while frying or pull apart gently with fork and spatula until well shredded.

Serves: 2

ORIENTAL PEPPER STEAK

Ingredients:
1 pound round steak

1/4 cup soy sauce

1 green pepper, sliced

1 clove garlic

1 teaspoon brown sugar

1/2 teaspoon ginger

2 tablespoons cooking oil

1/2 cup mushrooms, sliced

Directions:
Thinly slice steak across grain. Place in a bowl. Add soy sauce, green pepper, garlic, sugar and ginger. Marinate 2 hours. Drain. Heat oil over medium heat. Add steak, peppers and mushrooms. Stir-fry for 4 minutes or until meat is cooked.

Serves: 4

VAGABOND FINGER STEAKS

Ingredients:

3 to 3 1/2 pounds
round steak, cut
1 1/2 to 2 inches
thick
1 large onion, sliced
1 (8 ounce) can sliced
mushrooms
Seasoned meat
tenderizer
1 tablespoon vinegar
2 tablespoons butter or
margarine

Directions:

Prepare meat with meat tenderizer as directed
on the package. With a sharp knife, slice meat
across the grain at a slight angle into thin
strips. Heat butter or margarine in cast-iron
skillet on grill; add onions; sauté until just
tender. Add meat strips and brown quickly,
about 2 1/2 minutes. Do not overcook. Add
mushrooms and vinegar, blend well. Cover
and simmer for 5 minutes or until heated
through.

Serves: 6

BROILED LAMB CHOPS

Ingredients:

6 lamb chops, center
cut, 1-inch thick
2 teaspoons garlic salt
2 teaspoons oregano

Directions:

Sprinkle chops with garlic salt and oregano.
Place in baking pan and broil 6 minutes. Turn
chops and broil 6 minutes more.

Serves: 4 to 6

BREADED STUFFED LAMB CHOPS

Ingredients:
4 lamb chops, 1 1/2
   inches thick (Have
   butcher cut pockets
   in chops for stuffing)
Salt and pepper to taste
2 cups bread stuffing
1 1/4 cups bread
   crumbs, seasoned
1 egg, beaten

Directions:
Season chops by rubbing with salt and pepper both inside cut pocket and outside. Evenly stuff each chop with stuffing. Coat with bread crumbs, egg, then once again with bread crumbs. Arrange in large baking pan. Place in a 450°F oven for 20 minutes. Turn and bake 20 minutes more.

Serves: 6

LEG OF LAMB A LA ELLEN

Ingredients:
1 (4-5 pound) leg of
   lamb, rolled and tied
3 or 4 cloves garlic,
   sliced thin
1 (2 ounce) can flat
   anchovy filets,
drained and halved
   crosswise
1 1/2 teaspoon
   rosemary, dried
Pepper to taste

Directions:
Make 2-inch deep cuts in lamb 1-inch apart. Push garlic and anchovies alternately into incisions. Rub outside of lamb with rosemary and pepper. Bake at 325°F for 1 1/2 hours.

Serves: 4 to 5

CANDIED LAMB CUBES

Ingredients:
1/4 cup cooking oil
3 pounds lamb cubes
2 tablespoons brown sugar
3 tablespoons flour
1 tablespoon lemon juice

Directions:
Place cooking oil in frying pan. Heat oil over medium-high heat. Add lamb cubes a few at a time and brown on all sides. Reduce heat to medium. Sprinkle sugar over lamb. Stir until sugar dissolves and liquid in pan browns. Add flour and lemon juice. Continue cooking, stirring constantly until lamb is well coated and juice is thick and bubbly.

Serves: 4 to 6

HERBED LAMB

Ingredients:
1 teaspoon dried basil
1 teaspoon thyme
1 teaspoon marjoram
1 teaspoon salt
6 loin lamb chops, 1 inch thick

Directions:
Combine basil, thyme, marjoram and salt, and rub this mixture into the lamb chops. Cover and refrigerate chops for 1 1/2 hours. Turn the oven on to broil, place the chops on a broiler pan or on a rack in a baking pan, and set the pan in the oven 6 inches from the heat. Broil 6 minutes on each side.

Serves: 4 to 6

IRISH STEW

Ingredients:
2 pounds boneless lamb
   cubes
1 potato, cubed
1/2 cup cubed carrots
2 cups sliced potatoes
1/2 cup cubed turnips
Salt and pepper
1 onion, sliced

Directions:
Cover lamb cubes with boiling water, cover, and simmer 1 hour. Add turnips, carrots, onion and the cubed potato. Cover and simmer 1/2 hour. Add the sliced potato. Cover and simmer 1/2 hour and season to taste with the salt and pepper.

Serves: 6

LAMB CHOPS A LA MUSHROOMS

Ingredients:
- 2 tablespoons butter or margarine
- 4 lamb chops, 1 inch thick
- 1 can mushroom soup, condensed
- 1/2 cup mushrooms
- 1/2 cup water
- Salt and pepper to taste

Directions:
Melt butter or margarine in skillet. Add chops and fry 7 minutes on each side or until browned. Meanwhile, combine soup, mushrooms and water in bowl. Stir and set aside. Remove chops to baking dish. Pour soup mixture over top. Bake in a 350°F oven for 20 minutes.

Serves: 4

QUICK-FRY LAMB

Ingredients:
- 2 tablespoons cooking oil
- 1 clove garlic, minced
- 1 pound lamb, cut into 2-inch cubes
- 5 scallions, chopped
- 1/2 cup bean sprouts
- 2 tablespoons soy sauce

Directions:
Heat skillet or wok with cooking oil. Add garlic and simmer 30 seconds. Add lamb and simmer 2 minutes or until pink is gone. Add scallions, sprouts and soy sauce. Stir until heated through about 3 minutes. Scallions will be crisp.

Serves: 4

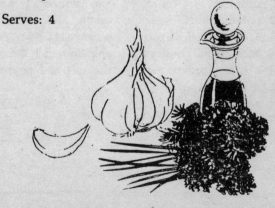

MINTED LAMB STEAKS

Ingredients:
4 cups cold water
1 teaspoon cornstarch
4 teaspoons dried mint
   flakes, crushed
1 tablespoon corn syrup
1/2 teaspoon shredded
   lemon peel
1/4 teaspoon salt
4 lamb steaks, about
   3/4 inch thick

Directions:
For glaze: In saucepan combine water and cornstarch. Add mint, corn syrup, lemon peel and salt. Cook and stir until thick and bubbly. Place steaks on unheated rack or broiler pan. Broil 3 to 4 inches from heat for 5 minutes. Brush some glaze over steaks. Turn steaks; broil 5 to 6 minutes more, brushing occasionally with glaze.

Serves: 4

ROASTED LAMB CHOPS

Ingredients:
6 lamb chops, 2 1/2
   inches thick
12 bacon strips
Salt and pepper to taste
3 tablespoons flour

Directions:
Wrap lamb chops with bacon strips. Sprinkle with salt, pepper and flour. Place in lightly oiled skillet and brown well on both sides. Remove from skillet and place on rack in roasting pan. Place in a 350°F oven and roast 20 minutes or until tender.

Serves: 4 to 6

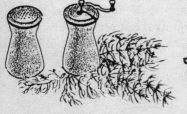

CREAMED SAUSAGE ON MUFFINS

Ingredients:

1/2 pound sausage, without casing
1 small onion, sliced
2 tablespoons cornstarch
1 1/2 cups milk
3 English muffins, split in half

Directions:

Brown sausage in skillet, crumbling into small pieces. Reduce heat and drain. Stirring constantly, add flour and simmer until thickened. Add milk, bring to a boil and reduce heat. Simmer, stirring once again until thickened. Scoop over bottom half of English muffins. Place tops over mixture to make sandwiches.

Serves: 3

FRENCH FRANKS

Ingredients:
8 French rolls
Garlic butter
Chopped chives
Chopped parsley
8 frankfurters, grilled
8 slices cheese
Barbecue sauce

Directions:
Spread French rolls with garlic butter to which you have added some chopped chives and parsley. Add grilled frankfurters and slices of cheese. Wrap each frank and roll in foil and heat until the cheese melts. Serve with a bowl of hot barbecue sauce for dunking.

Serves: 4

FUN FRANKFURTERS

Ingredients:
1 tablespoon butter or margarine
1 medium onion, sliced thin
1 cup chilli sauce
2 tablespoons pickle relish
1 tablespoon brown sugar
1 tablespoon prepared mustard
6 frankfurters

Directions:
Melt butter or margarine in large skillet. Add onions and simmer until onions are clear. In bowl, combine chilli sauce, relish, brown sugar and mustard. Pour in skillet. Add franks, stir and cover. Simmer 10 minutes, stirring occasionally. Remove franks to platter and pour sauce over top. *Options:* Slice franks in halves or smaller. Serve on hot dog rolls, spooning sauce mixture over top. Cooked sausage or pork chops also work well in this recipe. *Helpful Hints:* Serve with french fries or corn-on-the-cob.

Serves: 6

HEARTY SAUSAGE DELUXE

Ingredients:

1 pound small sausage links
1 (28 ounce) can whole tomatoes, undrained
1 bay leaf
1 bouillon cube, beef
1/2 teaspoon thyme
Salt and pepper to taste
1 (10 ounce) package frozen mixed vegetables, thawed

Directions:

In large skillet brown sausage links evenly on all sides. Drain excess fat. In bowl combine tomatoes, bay leaf, bouillon cubes, thyme, salt and pepper. Stir, mashing tomatoes lightly. Pour over sausages. Stir gently scraping bottom of pan. Cover and simmer 35 minutes or until the liquid in the pan thickens. Remove bay leaf. Add vegetables and heat thoroughly.

Serves: 4

SAUSAGE SCALLOPINI

Ingredients:

1 pound sausage, without casing
1 green pepper, chopped
1 onion, chopped
1/2 cup mushrooms, sliced
1 (8 ounce) can tomatoes, drained

Directions:

Form sausage into 6 to 8 patties. Arrange in skillet. Over medium heat, brown sausage, frying 8 minutes on each side. Drain. Add pepper and onion. Sauté over medium-low heat 8 minutes or until lightly brown. Stir occasionally. Add mushrooms and tomatoes. Cover and simmer 10 minutes.

Serves: 4

SAUSAGE STEW

Ingredients:

1/4 pound link sausage, cut into 1/2-inch rounds

4 medium potatoes, peeled, cut into cubes

3 cups water

1/2 pound spinach, chopped

1 clove garlic, minced

Salt and pepper to taste

Directions:

Place sausage in saucepan. Simmer over medium heat 7 minutes or until evenly browned. Drain excess oil. Add potatoes, water, spinach, garlic, salt and pepper. Stir, scraping bottom to loosen bits. Bring to boil, cover and simmer 20 minutes or until potatoes are tender. *Options:* Use pieces of beef, veal or chicken. Add grated cheese or mushrooms. Substitute water with canned tomatoes. Use fresh or frozen spinach. *Helpful Hints:* Serve with buttered biscuits, rolls or garlic bread.

Serves: 2 to 4

SPICY HOT SAUSAGE AND PEPPERS

Ingredients:

1 tablespoon cooking oil

1 pound sausage, hot

1 green pepper, cut into chunks

1 medium onion, sliced

1 (16 ounce) can tomatoes, undrained

Directions:

Heat cooking oil in large skillet. Cut sausage into 1-inch pieces and add to skillet. Brown sausage lightly and remove from pan. Drain excess fat. Add pepper and onion. Sauté, stirring occasionally, until just tender. Return sausage to skillet. Stir in tomatoes. Cover and simmer over low heat 25 minutes or until liquid in skillet evaporates.

Serves: 2 to 4

BAKED LIVER AND BACON

Ingredients:
1 pound liver
8 bacon strips
1 cup water
Salt and pepper to taste

Directions:
Place liver in baking dish. Lay strips of bacon over top. Add 1 cup water. Cover and bake in a 350°F oven 40 minutes or until liver is tender. Remove liver from baking dish, keeping bacon strips over top. Season with salt and pepper.

Serves: 2 to 4

LOW CALORIE BROILED LIVER

Ingredients:
2 to 3 pounds liver
2 tablespoons butter or margarine
Salt and pepper to taste

Directions:
Place liver into broiler for 5 minutes, turning often. Remove liver from pan and dot with butter or margarine, salt and pepper.

Serves: 2 to 4

SAUTÉED CHICKEN LIVERS

Ingredients:
2 slices bacon, cut up
1 small onion, chopped
2 tablespoons butter or margarine
1 pound chicken livers
1 cup chicken broth
1 teaspoon lemon juice
2 tablespoons flour

Directions:
In large skillet, fry bacon until lightly brown. Remove bacon and set aside. Drain excess fat from skillet. Add onion and butter. Sauté until onions are transparent. Add chicken livers and sauté 2 minutes. Mix broth, lemon juice, flour and bacon until lumps disappear. Pour in skillet. Sauté 5 minutes more, stirring, until mixture thickens and is bubbly.

Serves: 4

SAUTÉED LIVER OVER RICE

Ingredients:
2 pounds liver
1 egg, beaten
1/2 cup bread crumbs
2 tablespoons butter or margarine
1 medium onion, sliced thick
1/2 cup mushrooms, sliced
4 tablespoons white wine
Salt and pepper to taste
2 cups rice, cooked

Directions:
With sharp knife, slice liver into 1-inch cubes. Coat cubes with beaten egg, then bread crumbs. Heat butter or margarine in skillet. Place cubes into heated butter and brown evenly on all sides. Add more butter, if needed. Add onions, mushrooms, wine, salt and pepper. Simmer, covered 15 minutes or until onions and mushrooms are tender. Serve over mounds of hot, cooked rice.

Serves: 4 to 6

BAKED HAM SLICES WITH TOMATOES

Ingredients:
8 thick slices smoked ham, about 4 pounds
2 (14 1/2 ounce) cans tomatoes
1/4 teaspoon salt
1/4 teaspoon pepper
1/2 pound sliced American cheese

Directions:
Place ham slices in shallow baking dish. Drain 1 can tomatoes and combine with other can of undrained tomatoes. Break tomatoes up into halves or smaller pieces. Add salt and pepper to tomatoes. Pour mixture over ham. Cover and bake in preheated 350°F oven 20 minutes. Cut cheese slices in strips and arrange over ham slices. Return dish to oven for 10 to 15 minutes or until cheese is melted and browned.

Serves: 8

PORK POT PIE

Ingredients:

2 cups pork, cooked,
   diced

1/2 cup potatoes,
   peeled, diced

1/4 cup carrots, diced

Water, enough to just
   cover mixture in
   saucepan, plus 3
   tablespoons

2 beef bouillon cubes

Salt and pepper to taste

2 tablespoons flour

1/4 cup peas, cooked,
   drained

1 tablespoon margarine

Plain pastry dough,
   enough to cover
   top of pie

Directions:

Place pork, potatoes and carrots in saucepan. Add enough water to cover mixture. Bring to boil. Reduce heat and add bouillon cubes, salt and pepper. Cover and simmer 30 minutes or until vegetables are just tender. Mix flour with 3 tablespoons water until a smooth paste forms. Stir flour mixture and peas into saucepan. Simmer, stirring constantly, until thick and bubbly. Meanwhile, coat a 7 x 9 inch baking pan with margarine. Prepare pastry dough according to directions. Roll and flatten with rolling pin to shape of your pan. Pour mixture into pan and lay dough over top. Pinch edges all around to secure crust. Poke top of dough with fork a few times. Place in a 450°F oven 15 minutes or until top is golden brown. *Options:* Use any precooked vegetable you may desire. This recipe calls for a single layer of dough for over top of pie but if you desire an inside crust, follow same directions and place another layer of dough inside baking pan before adding mixture.

Serves: 6

PATIO MARINATED HAM STEAK

Ingredients:
1 ham steak,
   1 1/2-2 1/2 inches
   thick
1 cup pineapple juice
1/4 cup sherry
1 teaspoon dry mustard
Worcestershire sauce

Directions:
Marinate ham steak in pineapple juice for at least 4 hours. Add sherry, dry mustard, and a few dashes of Worcestershire sauce. Grill slowly over coal at low heat about 40 to 60 minutes or until tender and well cooked. Baste steak with marinade several times during cooking.

Serves: 2 to 3

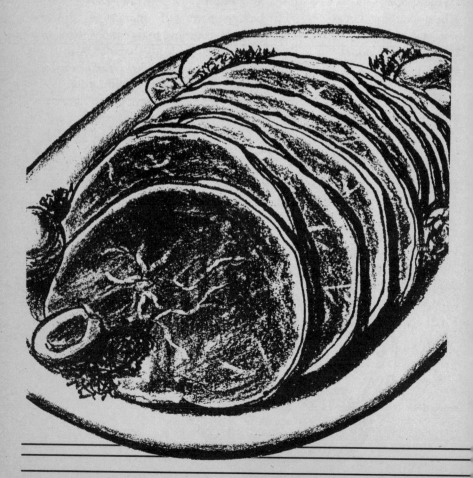

GERMAN PORK CHOPS

Ingredients:
- 4 pork chops, about 1/2-inch thick
- 2 tablespoons cooking oil
- 1/2 cup water
- 2 stalks celery, cut into 1-inch pieces
- 1 medium onion, chopped
- 1 clove garlic, minced
- 1 teaspoon paprika
- Salt to taste
- 1 cup sour cream

Directions:

Place chops in heated cooking oil and brown lightly on both sides. Stir in water, celery, onion, garlic, paprika and salt. Reduce heat, cover and simmer 1 hour or until chops are tender. Remove chops from skillet. Add sour cream and stir until well blended. Return chops to skillet and cover. Simmer 7 minutes or until mixture is thoroughly heated through.

Serves: 4

GLAZED APPLES AND PORK

Ingredients:
- 2 tablespoons butter or margarine
- 1/4 cup honey
- 8 boneless smoked pork chops
- 1/4 cup cranberry-orange relish
- 1 (20 ounce) can sliced apples

Directions:

Melt butter in a large skillet over moderate heat (about 250°F). Add pork chops and brown about 5 minutes on each side. Push chops to one side of skillet. Combine honey and cranberry-orange relish in the skillet; add apples and toss to coat with mixture. Cook about 5 minutes longer to heat apple mixture.

Serves: 4

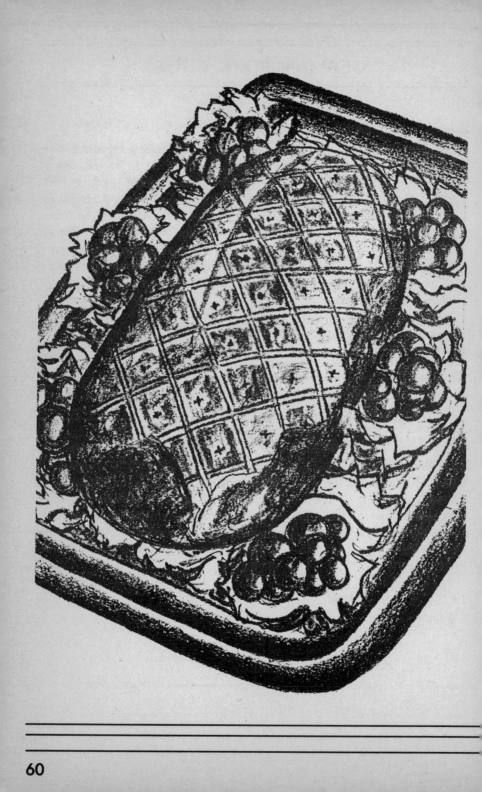

HAM SLICE WITH RICE

Ingredients:
1 1/2 pounds fully
  cooked, smoked ham,
  sliced 1-inch thick
3 cups hot, cooked rice
1/2 cup raisins
1 cup sour cream
1/3 cup sliced green
  onions
2 tablespoons mustard

Directions:
Place ham in center of ungreased baking dish. Mix sour cream and mustard in bowl; stir in rice, raisins and onions. Spoon rice mixture around ham. Cover and cook in 325°F oven 15 minutes. Uncover and cook until hot, 10 to 15 minutes longer.

Serves: 6

HOLIDAY SMOKED HAM

Ingredients:
1 2-2 1/2 pound
  smoked ham
Water
Prepared mustard
Whole cloves
Brown sugar

Directions:
Place ham in a deep kettle. Cover with cold water. Bring just to boiling. Do not boil. Simmer for 45 to 60 minutes per pound or until tender. Remove from water. Place in a shallow pan. Spread ham with prepared mustard. Stud with whole cloves. Sprinkle top of ham with brown sugar. Bake at 350°F about 30 minutes or until glazed.

Serves: 8

GOURMET GRILLED PORK CHOPS

Ingredients:
1/2 teaspoon rosemary
1/4 teaspoon thyme
1 tablespoon soy sauce
1/4 teaspoon sage
2 teaspoons corn oil
1/4 teaspoon garlic powder
1/2 teaspoon seasoned salt
6 pork chops, 3/4 inches thick

Directions:
Crush rosemary and combine with remaining ingredients except pork, mixing well. Brush mixture on chops. Grill chops 6 inches from coals; sear on both sides. Raise grill. Grill slowly 35 minutes or until well done, brushing chops occasionally with sauce.

Serves: 6

GROUND PORK BARBECUE

Ingredients:
1 pound ground pork
1 small onion, chopped
1 tablespoon cooking oil
1 cup bottled barbecue sauce
1 tablespoon Worcestershire sauce
Salt and pepper to taste
6 hamburger buns

Directions:
Place pork, onion and oil in skillet. Simmer over medium heat until pork browns. Drain excess oil. Stir in barbecue sauce, Worcestershire sauce, salt and pepper. Cover and simmer 10 minutes or until tender. Serve on hamburger buns. *Options:* Use ground beef, if desired. Add green pepper for added flavor. Tomato sauce can be used in place of barbecue sauce. *Helpful Hints:* A great change of pace instead of hamburgers or Sloppy Joes.

Serves: 4 to 6

INDEX